JESUS >
RELIGION
STUDENT BIBLE STUDY

LifeWay Press®
Nashville, Tennessee

Published by LifeWay Press® • © 2014 Jefferson Bethke
Reprinted Dec. 2014

ISBN: 9781430039723
Item number: P005720369

Dewey Decimal Classification Number: 248.83
Subject Heading: JESUS CHRIST \ CHRISTIAN LIFE \ GRACE (THEOLOGY)

Printed in the United States of America

Student Ministry Publishing
LifeWay Church Resources
One LifeWay Plaza
Nashville, TN 37234-0144

We believe that the Bible has God for its author; salvation for its end;
and truth, without any mixture of error, for its matter
and that all Scripture is totally true and trustworthy.
To review LifeWay's doctrinal guideline,
please visit *www.lifeway.com/doctrinalguideline.*

contents

ABOUT JEFFERSON BETHKE

HEY, GUYS! The first time meeting someone is always awkward, so I thought I'd start by sharing a little bit about myself.

I was born in Tacoma, Washington.
I played baseball in college.
I graduated with a degree in politics and government.
I co-own a company called Claro Candles, which donates its profits to combat injustice around the world.
I have a dog named Aslan (for Narnia!).
I'm married to an amazing, beautiful, sweet woman of God: Alyssa.
I'm a dad! Kinsley Joy Bethke is my sweet little daughter.
I wrote a book (so surreal!).
I like to make creative videos.

Enough about me. I'd love to hear about you and your story as it pertains to our Bible study together. Feel free to share, critique, question, or just say hello. My contact information is below. And use **#JesusIsGreater** to share any thoughts with the world.

TWITTER *www.twitter.com/jeffersonbethke*
INSTAGRAM *www.instagram.com/jeffersonbethke*
PINTEREST *www.pinterest.com/jeffersonbethke*

FACEBOOK *www.facebook.com/jeffersonbethkepage*
YOUTUBE *www.youtube.com/bball1989*
BLOG *www.jeffbethke.com*

For more on this subject, consider reading ***Jesus > Religion: Why He is so Much Better than Trying Harder, Doing More, and Being Good Enough*** by Jefferson Bethke (Nelson Books, 2013, ISBN 978-1-4002-0539-4).

HOW TO USE

Jesus > Religion is a six-session Bible study. Most groups meet weekly, completing one session a week, but feel free to follow a plan that meets the needs and schedule of your students.

Each session of *Jesus > Religion* consists of two major aspects of the study—group and personal. The leader guide will enable you to facilitate meaningful group discussion and challenge students to respond to what they are learning. The group content is arranged into the following sections:

> *Start* = This page includes questions to get the conversation started and to introduce the video segment.
> *Watch* = This page includes key points and Scripture references from Jeff's teaching.
> *Consider* = These pages include the bulk of the biblical content, including focal passages and context. Discussion questions are marked in bold and are the same in both the student book and leader guide. Ask these questions in the large group setting or divide your students into smaller groups to discuss at a deeper level.
> *Respond* = This page includes questions and statements to help your group respond to and apply what they are learning.

In addition to the group content, the student book includes Personal Reading and Reflection pages that dive deeper into passages pertaining to the main message of each session. Encourage your students to work through these 3 devotions during the week between group meetings. For those who want to read more on any particular topic, the opening page of each Personal Reading & Reflection section highlights related chapters from the book *Jesus > Religion: Why He is so Much Better than Trying Harder, Doing More, and Being Good Enough* by Jefferson Bethke (Nelson Books, 2013, ISBN 978-1-4002-0539-4).

GROUP LEADER TIPS

> Prayerfully prepare by reviewing the material and praying for each person in your group.
> Minimize distractions for your group meetings.
> Encourage discussion within your group. Ensure everyone has a chance to participate.
> Stay connected. Follow up with students via text, social media, or personal interaction.

session one
JESUS>RELIGION

start

Welcome everyone to the first group session. Depending on the size of your group, divide students into smaller groups or keep everyone together and ask them to answer the following questions:

When have you been surprised by something that turned out better than you expected?

Reflect on a time when you missed out on something great or found yourself in an awkward situation because of a misunderstanding?

Over the next six weeks students will be challenged to set aside their preconceived ideas about religion and honestly consider (or reconsider) the person of Jesus. Challenge students to keep the following question in mind as they begin this study and watch the "Jesus > Religion" video:

WHAT IF LIFE WITH JESUS IS BETTER THAN YOU THOUGHT?

watch

View Session One "Jesus > Religion" video from the Leader Kit. Encourage students to focus on the video during this time and use the *Watch* section of the student book to reference Scripture and main points Jeff shares in the video segment.

REMEMBER THIS 🎧

> Christianity is not about us coming to God. It's about God coming to us.
> Rules and institutions are beautiful when they are a response to a relationship.
> We all struggle. We're all frail, broken, messed-up people.
> We're all looking to be known, to be loved, and to have purpose. Only Jesus can provide that.

THINK ABOUT THIS ❓

How would your life be different if you really understood that Jesus is the only One who can give you joy, hope, peace, and life?

LOOK IT UP 📖

> Hebrews 3:1, 4:14, 7:27
> 1 Corinthians 3:16
> Revelation 21:22
> Psalm 32:9
> Isaiah 30:16
> John 1:14
> 1 Peter 2:24
> Ephesians 2:1
> Romans 3:10-12, 4:5, 7:18-19

consider

What does being a Christian mean to you? Explain.

Let's look to the ultimate source for understanding Christianity and make sure our view lines up with the Bible.

Call on a volunteer to read Ephesians 2:4-10.

> **LEADER NOTES //** "We were dead in our sins, but God ... " "God could have left us spiritually dead, in rebellion against him and in bondage to our sins. But he didn't. In the previous verses Paul wrote about our old sinful nature (Eph. 2:1-3). Here Paul emphasizes that we do not need to live any longer under sin's power. The penalty of sin and its power over us were miraculously destroyed by Christ on the cross. Through faith in Christ we stand acquitted, or not guilty, before God." [1]

What aspects of God's character stand out in these verses?

What do these verses say about Jesus?

Call on a volunteer to read Romans 8:10-11.

> **LEADER NOTES //** When we become a child of God, His Spirit takes up residence inside us. We become the temple where His presence dwells. Our physical bodies will one day die as a result of sin, but the Spirit breathes life into us for all our days on earth and seals us for eternity. We have hope for this life and the life to come because of Jesus Christ. [2]

According to this passage, what is our hope based on?

What earthly things have you placed your hope and happiness in? What is the danger of putting your hope in anyone or anything besides Jesus?

Call on a volunteer to read Romans 4:4-5.

LEADER NOTES // Salvation is a free gift of God. He justifies the ungodly and draws sinners to Himself through the power of the gospel. Those who trust in the work of Christ to save them recognize that they could do nothing to earn His grace. Restoration and freedom comes by faith in what He has already done on our behalf. In Him, we are made righteous. [3]

How does the fact that God justifies the ungodly give you freedom in life?

Are you encouraged to hear that the Bible is full of broken, messed up people who were loved and changed by God's grace? Explain.

What else did Jeff say in the video that was encouraging, convicting, or helpful?

respond

Challenge students to think about how the truth discussed in this session impacts their lives. Point them to the *Respond* section of the student book and encourage them to write their thoughts. If time permits, allow them to share what they wrote with the group.

Jeff shared that he tried religion and walked away from it, only to realize that he misunderstood Jesus and what being a Christian is really about.

Is your understanding of Christianity centered on religion or a relationship with Jesus? Explain.

session two
LOVE>SELF

start

Allow time for students to share any questions or thoughts they have from this week's personal reading and reflection pages.

Encourage a student to read aloud the opening paragraph found on page 18 in the student book. Depending on the size of your group, divide students into smaller groups or keep everyone together and ask them to answer the following questions:

How often are you tempted to compare yourself to others? When is the last time you remember doing so?

Are you more likely to compare yourself to people you think are better than you? Or to those you feel you are better than? Why?

It is human nature to constantly make comparisons. Challenge students to keep the following question in mind as they watch the "Love > Self" video:

DO YOU LOOK TO JESUS OR TO PEOPLE WHEN MEASURING YOUR WORTH?

watch

View Session Two "Love > Self" video from the Leader Kit. Encourage students to focus on the video during this time and use the *Watch* section of the student book to reference Scripture and main points Jeff shares in the video segment.

REMEMBER THIS 🎧

> When you make something other than Jesus central, that's idolatry.
> Comparison is an endless cycle.
> God doesn't grade on a curve; He grades on a cross.
> God has rescued us through the person and work of Jesus.

THINK ABOUT THIS ❓

> Do you understand that Jesus doesn't go around you, He goes straight to you?
> In light of the grace you've been given, do you point others to grace?

LOOK IT UP 📖

> John 4:1-42
> Ephesians 6:12
> Colossians 1:21
> Romans 5:10
> 2 Corinthians 5:21
> Hebrews 4:15
> Matthew 22:36-40

consider

Let's begin with the questions Jeff asked at the end of the video:

How have you experienced the cycle of disappointment that occurs when you compare yourself to others?

What do you think Jeff meant when he said, "God doesn't grade on a curve; He grades on a cross?"

How have you experienced God's grace? In what ways have you shared it with others?

Call on a volunteer to read John 4:1-30.

LEADER NOTES // In Jesus' day, Jews and Samaritans were bitter rivals. Often, Jews would journey around Samaria to avoid any interaction with Samaritans. But Jesus reached beyond cultural and religious barriers to extend His grace. In this account, Jesus met a Samaritan woman who was living in sin and offered her forgiveness and freedom. Through her testimony of faith, an entire village was transformed.[4]

Why do you think Jesus went through Samaria instead of going around it?

What struggles in your life or in the lives of others seem too sinful for Jesus to change?

Jeff pointed out that people often demonize the opposite of what they idolize. In other words, people are threatened by anything or anyone in competition with what they love. So much so, that they often attempt to discredit or make the other side look wicked in some way or another.

How have you seen people demonize the opposite of what they idolize?

How does grace change the endless cycle of comparison?

respond

Challenge students to think about how the truth discussed in this session impacts their lives. Point them to the *Respond* section of the student book and encourage them to write their thoughts. If time permits, allow them to share what they wrote with the group.

Consider the fact that Jesus doesn't go around you, He's not afraid of your sin, and He comes to you right where you are.

How does that reality bring you hope? Explain.

session three
GIVER>GIFTS

start

Allow time for students to share any questions or thoughts they have from this week's personal reading and reflection pages.

Remind students that session two focused on grace, humility, and love. Let them know that in this session, we'll shift our focus to blessings and joy. Depending on the size of your group, divide students into smaller groups or keep everyone together and ask them to answer the following questions:

What is the greatest gift you have ever received? Why?

Is there anything in your life that you'd be devastated by if it was lost or taken? Explain.

Sometimes we value something in and of itself. Other times—and most often with gifts—the value of something is enhanced by the relationship of the person who gave it to us or the history behind it. Challenge students to keep the following question in mind as they watch the "Giver > Gifts" video:

DO YOU LOVE JESUS FOR WHO HE IS OR FOR WHAT YOU HOPE TO GET OUT OF THE DEAL?

watch

View Session Three "Giver > Gifts" video from the Leader Kit. Encourage students to focus on the video during this time and use the *Watch* section of the student book to reference Scripture and main points Jeff shares in the video segment.

REMEMBER THIS

> The root of sin in our lives is idolatry.
> Anything other than Jesus is an idol.
> God is saying these things about idolatry because He wants to give us the most joy possible.
> When your hope and identity is in the Creator, true joy is found.

THINK ABOUT THIS

> If everything in your life was taken away, would Jesus be enough for you?
> Are you following God to get His gifts or to get Him?

LOOK IT UP

> Romans 1:25, 8:35-39
> James 1:17
> Exodus 20:1-17
> John 10:10, 15:11
> Matthew 6:19-21
> Hebrews 6:17-20, 12:28
> Ephesians 1:3

consider

Let's begin with some questions Jeff asked in the video

If everything in your life were taken away, would Jesus be enough? Explain.

When have you tried to use God to get things you wanted?

Call on a volunteer to read Matthew 6:19-21.

> **LEADER NOTES //** "We are accustomed to dividing life into the 'spiritual' and the "material"; but Jesus made no such division. In many of His parables, He made it clear that a right attitude toward wealth is a mark of true spirituality (see Luke 12:13; 16:1-31). The Pharisees were covetous (Luke 16:14) and used religion to make money. If we have the true righteousness of Christ in our lives, then we will have a proper attitude toward material wealth." [5]

What does Jesus teach about the source of our hope and happiness?

Call on a volunteer to read Romans 8:35-39.

> **LEADER NOTES //** Once we belong to Jesus, nothing can ever separate us from Him. This is a comforting promise in light of the reality that we will surely face hardships in this life. The sacrifice of Christ on our behalf is proof of His immeasurable love. The resurrection is proof of His power to keep His promises. We are secure in Christ, no matter our circumstances. Our lives, both here and for eternity, are safe in His hands. We need not fear persecution, illness, or even death. His presence is our refuge. [6]

What encouragement do these verses provide about the love of Jesus and your circumstances?

Call on a volunteer to read James 1:17.

LEADER NOTES // When we focus on the gift instead of the Giver, we can easily be convinced that God is holding out on us if we don't get what we desire or pray for. The enemy will always try to twist the words of God in an attempt to make us question His character. God is perfect in all His ways and His goodness to us is beyond our ability to comprehend. We must keep our hearts set on Him and trust in His ability to meet our every need. [7]

When do you most often focus on gifts instead of the Giver?

How can you focus on the Giver instead of just gifts? List some steps you can take to help shift your focus today.

Call on a volunteer to read John 10:10 and 15:11.

LEADER NOTES // The thief is set on destruction. His purpose is to steal, kill and destroy. But Jesus offers life that is rich and abundant. His grace brings freedom that floods our hearts with joy. The gift of salvation is everlasting, but begins immediately when we enter into a relationship with Christ by faith. Our Savior has overcome the thief so we never have to live in fear or bondage to the schemes of the enemy.[8]

What does Jesus want to give us?

respond

Challenge students to think about how the truth discussed in this session impacts their lives. Point them to the *Respond* section of the student book and encourage them to write their thoughts. If time permits, allow them to share what they wrote with the group.

How would you answer the question Jeff asked in the video: "What's the point of following Jesus?"

session four
COVENANT >
CONTRACT

start

Remind students that session three focused on idolatry, God as Father, and hope. Ask the following:

What was most helpful, encouraging, or challenging from your personal reading and reflection this past week?

Let students know that in this session, we'll take an even deeper look at our relationship with God through Christ. Depending on the size of your group, divide students into smaller groups or keep everyone together and ask them to answer the following questions:

What is the most meaningful promise anyone has ever kept to you?

What is the worst experience you've ever had with a broken promise?

Relationships are built on trust. We know that everyone is imperfect—we'll let others down and we'll be let down. But Jesus is always faithful. Challenge students to keep the following question in mind as they watch the "Covenant > Contract" video:

WHAT DOES A RELATIONSHIP WITH JESUS LOOK LIKE?

watch

View Session Four "Covenant > Contract" video from the Leader Kit. Encourage students to focus on the video during this time and use the *Watch* section of the student book to reference Scripture and main points Jeff shares in the video segment.

REMEMBER THIS 💬

> A covenant is about the promise, not the behavior.
> A contract is about the behavior, not a promise.
> To be a Christian is about identity, not activity. Activity flows from that identity.
> Coming to Jesus is the beginning of the road, not the end.
> You are a child of the living God, under covenant, not contract.

THINK ABOUT THIS ❓

> Do you believe that God celebrates when you come home?
> Do you understand that you are a child of the living God who is under covenant, not contract?

LOOK IT UP 📖

> Luke 15:1-2, 11-32
> Matthew 23:23
> Romans 1:25
> Deuteronomy 7:9
> Genesis 3:8-9

consider

Do you believe you are accepted and loved unconditionally by God as His child? Or do you live with the fear that one day He may give up on you?

When have you felt you were one sin away from God giving up on you?

Call on a volunteer to read Luke 15:1-2.

LEADER NOTES // "The religious leaders were always careful to stay 'clean' according to Old Testament law. By contrast, Jesus took their concept of "cleanness" lightly. He risked defilement by touching those who had leprosy and by neglecting to wash in the Pharisees' prescribed manner, and he showed complete disregard for their sanctions against associating with certain classes of people. He came to offer salvation to sinners and to show that God loves them. Jesus didn't worry about the accusations. Instead, he continued going to those who needed him, regardless of the effect these rejected people might have on his reputation." [9]

Religion makes enemies. Jesus makes friends. Throughout His earthly ministry, Jesus reached out to those who were rejected or marginalized.

What encouragement or conviction does it give you to know that Jesus reached out to sinners and they were drawn to Him?

Read Luke 15:11-32.

LEADER NOTES // The "Parable of the Prodigal Son" is a beautiful story about redemption, restoration, and the unconditional love of a father. The word prodigal means "wasteful" which describes the choices and lifestyle of the younger son and in many ways the older son as well. They both disregarded the relationship they had with the father. But the father was patient and generous with his love. It was the father's goodness that eventually brought the younger son home in an act of repentance. [10]

Are you more like the rebellious or entitled son in this story? Explain.

When have you experienced the grace of the Heavenly Father?

How does understanding that you're a child under covenant, not under contract, change your view of God?

How does it change your view of sin and forgiveness to know that your Father celebrates your return?

Jeff explained that the gospel isn't just for saving you. The gospel is relevant every day, especially when you mess up.

List some ways you need Jesus each day.

Call on a volunteer to read Genesis 3:8-9.

LEADER NOTES // "The thought of two humans covered with fig leaves trying to hide from the all-seeing, all-knowing God is humorous. Yet we do the same, acting as though God doesn't know what we're doing. Have the courage to share all you do and think with him. Honesty will strengthen your relationship with God." [11]

What was man's response to sin? God's response?

respond

Challenge students to think about how the truth discussed in this session impacts their lives. Point them to the *Respond* section of the student book and encourage them to write their thoughts. If time permits, allow them to share what they wrote with the group.

Starting right now, how can you come out of hiding, take off your mask, and experience the joy and freedom of Christ?

session five
WORSHIP >
RITUALS

start

Session four focused on freedom, family, and failure.

What was most helpful, encouraging, or challenging from your personal reading and reflection in session four?

Today, we'll begin looking at the practice of worship.

What do you think of when you hear the word *worship*?

There are certain elements or rituals that may be included in worship, but worship is more than just something done at a certain time or place. Challenge students to keep the following question in mind as they watch the "Worship > Rituals" video:

IF JESUS > RELIGION, WHAT DOES IT MEAN TO WORSHIP HIM?

watch

View Session Five "Worship > Rituals" video from the Leader Kit. Encourage students to focus on the video during this time and use the *Watch* section of the student book to reference Scripture and main points Jeff shares in the video segment.

REMEMBER THIS 💭

> Good things can be distorted when we worship them.
> We are to worship God in spirit and in truth.
> God is breaking down the wall between the secular and sacred.
> It's not about sacred space, but about people who worship God correctly.
> In Jesus, we become the true temple.
> All of life is worship.

THINK ABOUT THIS ❓

> Are you worshiping God correctly—in spirit and truth?
> Are you worshiping God in all of life?

LOOK IT UP 📖

> 2 Corinthians 5:18-19
> Genesis 1, 2:15
> Exodus 20:3-5
> John 4:20-24
> 1 Corinthians 6:19, 10:31, 12:4
> 2 Corinthians 6:16
> 1 Timothy 4:4
> Matthew 7:11, 28:19
> Revelation 21:10

consider

Where else, besides Jesus, do people seek meaning and purpose in life?

What have you lived for in the past?

When have you wondered or even worried about God's will?

How do our previous discussions about freedom and God as a loving Father help you understand that His will is more like the boundaries of a circle than a precise point we have to get right?

We can overcomplicate God's will and what's right, holy, or considered ministry. God's will is specific about our general purpose, but it allows freedom in the practical, everyday details.

Call on a volunteer to read 2 Corinthians 5:18-19.

LEADER NOTES // Though we were once God's enemies because of sin, we are reconciled (made right) with Him through faith in Christ. Redemption changes us from the inside out. Upon receiving God's grace, we are given the privilege and responsibility of encouraging others to be reconciled with God. This ministry of reconciliation becomes the heartbeat of our lives for the rest of our days on earth. [12]

What do these verses identify as God's general will for our lives?

Call on a volunteer to read 1 Corinthians 6:19-20 and 2 Corinthians 6:16.

LEADER NOTES // When we receive Christ as Savior, our bodies become a temple in which His Spirit abides and through which He accomplishes Kingdom work. We should keep our bodies holy because we've been bought with a price. We should desire to bring Him glory and honor through our thoughts, words and actions. [13]

How does being the temple of God influence the way you see your life?

What does it mean not to be your own?

How does being the temple shape your understanding of worship?

Call on a volunteer to read 1 Corinthians 10:31.

LEADER NOTES // We should do everything we do for the glory of God and the benefit of others. We are called to submit every aspect of our lives to Him and use our gifts, resources, and opportunities for His purposes. As believers, we let go of our rights to do whatever we want and we begin to live in such a way that others are drawn to Jesus through our words and actions. This is God's will for our lives. [14]

What do you enjoy doing?

How can you worship God in that pursuit?

respond

Challenge students to think about how the truth discussed in this session impacts their lives. Point them to the *Respond* section of the student book and encourage them to write their thoughts. If time permits, allow them to share what they wrote with the group.

How can you use your gifts, talents, and passions for God's glory?

COMMUNITY >
CONFORMITY

start

Session five focused on your calling, God's will, and worship.

What was most helpful, encouraging, or challenging from your personal reading and reflection in session five?

We'll begin with a look at life in community—which comes from the word "common."

What do you share in common with the students in this group? What are some differences?

In Jesus, what we have in common is greater than our differences. That is at the heart of community. The unity and diversity of the church should be a beautiful thing. Unfortunately, church is one of the most misunderstood parts of a relationship with Jesus, today.

Each session is intended to help students set aside preconceived ideas and experiences with things they may associate with religion—Jesus, the Bible, worship, holiness, etc. Challenge your students to keep the following question in mind as they watch the "Community > Conformity" video:

IF JESUS > RELIGION, WHY IS THE CHURCH SO IMPORTANT?

watch

View Session Six "Community > Conformity" video from the Leader Kit. Encourage students to focus on the video during this time and use the *Watch* section of the student book to reference Scripture and main points Jeff shares in the video segment.

REMEMBER THIS 🎧

> - You were created for community.
> - Trying to live without community is like trying to live without oxygen.
> - The church is God's agent to reconcile the world to Himself.
> - The church is the body of Christ. Jesus is the head of the body.
> - A body works best if everything is doing separate things pointing toward the greater cause.

THINK ABOUT THIS ❓

> - What if, instead of thinking we exist for our own benefit, we saw the church as existing for what it really is—the bride and body of Christ, showing His love and grace to all who need it.

LOOK IT UP 📖

> - Genesis 1:26
> - 2 Corinthians 5:19-20
> - Matthew 16:18
> - Acts 2:37-47
> - Galatians 3:28, 6:2
> - 1 Corinthians 12:4-6, 12-20, 25-26
> - Ephesians 2:13, 4:15, 5:25-27
> - Romans 12:10
> - Hebrews 10:24-25
> - Revelation 19:7

consider

Jeff opened the video saying that by God's design we're created for community.

Which illustration do you best relate to? Why?

◯ **Life without community is like life without oxygen.**
◯ **Life without community is like sitting on a one-legged stool.**
◯ **Life in community is like a family.**

The diversity of the early church was a scandalous community like the world had never seen.

Call on a volunteer to read 1 Corinthians 12:4-6, 12-20, 25-26, and Galatians 3:28.

LEADER NOTES // "The disunity among the believers in Corinth forced Paul to deal with this problem by expounding at length on the body metaphor. Believers in the church are the individual parts that make up Christ's body. All parts of Christ's body must work together for the body to function properly." In Galatians, Paul talks more about unity. "The equality and unity spoken of here is of a spiritual nature— in Christ. Paul had just discussed at length that the Jew has no spiritual advantage over the Greek (Gentile), and now he says the same equality is true for social and gender distinctions. No one people group or gender is to be exalted above others." [15]

What encouragement does Paul's description of diversity and unity give you as part of Jesus' body—His church?

Call on a volunteer to read Matthew 16:13-18.

LEADER NOTES // "Simon understood Jesus' identity due to divine revelation (Matt. 11:25-27), which is why Jesus nicknamed him Peter. Although Matthew previously referred to Simon as Peter, this is the first time in the Gospel that Jesus did so. Jesus identified Peter as the rock on which His church would be founded. Peter and the other apostles' proclamation of Jesus' messiahship laid the foundation for the church." [16]

Various opinions have always existed about Jesus' identity. Confessing the truth of Jesus as the Christ, the Son of God, is the common ground on which the church is built.

How would you explain to someone who Jesus is? How has this study helped you know and love Jesus more?

How would you explain what Jesus meant when He said the gates of hell wouldn't prevail against His church?

Call on a volunteer to read Romans 12:10, Galatians 6:2, and Hebrews 10:24-25.

LEADER NOTES // In each of these passages, believers are called to live in godly community—to love deeply, honor one another above ourselves and to carry each other's burdens. We are called to spend time together, encouraging and challenging one another to glorify God in our words and actions.

What actions are explicitly taught in each of these verses as characteristic of true Christian community?

When and how have you experienced this kind of community?

respond

Challenge students to think about how the truth discussed in this session impacts their lives. Point them to the *Respond* section of the student book and encourage them to write their thoughts. If time permits, allow them to share what they wrote with the group.

How can this group be that kind of community to one another?

CONCLUSION

As you wrap up this study, encourage students to articulate what they have learned or been challenged to consider over the last six weeks. Direct them to turn to page 77 in the student book and answer the following questions:

Is Jesus > Religion in your life? Explain.

How would you explain the difference between having religion and having a relationship with Jesus?

What are some key truths from this study that impacted your life?

How are you going to live differently because of what you have learned?

Allow students to share their answers with the whole group or with a partner. Close by praying for each participant by name.

If time permits, consider showing Jeff's spoken word poem entitled "Why I Hate Religion but Love Jesus." The video can be found at *www.youtube.com/bball1989*.

SOURCES

1 *Life Application Study Bible*, (Wheaton, IL: Tyndale, 1988), WORDsearch CROSS e-book, 2001.

2 Warren W. Wiersbe, *The Bible Exposition Commentary – New Testament, Volume 1*, (Colorado Springs, CO: Victor, 2001), WORDsearch CROSS e-book, 539.

3 *Life Application Study Bible*, (Wheaton, IL: Tyndale, 1988), WORDsearch CROSS e-book, 1900-1901.

4 Warren W. Wiersbe, *The Bible Exposition Commentary – New Testament, Volume 1*, (Colorado Springs, CO: Victor, 2001), WORDsearch CROSS e-book, 299.

5 Warren W. Wiersbe, *The Bible Exposition Commentary – New Testament, Volume 1*, (Colorado Springs, CO: Victor, 2001), WORDsearch CROSS e-book, 27.

6 *Life Application Study Bible*, (Wheaton, IL: Tyndale, 1988), WORDsearch CROSS e-book, 1909.

7 Warren W. Wiersbe, *The Bible Exposition Commentary – New Testament, Volume 2*, (Colorado Springs, CO: Victor, 2001), WORDsearch CROSS e-book, 343.

8 *Life Application Study Bible*, (Wheaton, IL: Tyndale, 1988), WORDsearch CROSS e-book, 1773.

9 *Life Application Study Bible*, (Wheaton, IL: Tyndale, 1988), WORDsearch CROSS e-book, 1719.

10 Warren W. Wiersbe, *The Bible Exposition Commentary – New Testament, Volume 1*, (Colorado Springs, CO: Victor, 2001), WORDsearch CROSS e-book, 234.

11 *Life Application Study Bible*, (Wheaton, IL: Tyndale, 1988), WORDsearch CROSS e-book, 10.

12 *Life Application Study Bible*, (Wheaton, IL: Tyndale, 1988), WORDsearch CROSS e-book, 1967.

13 *HCSB Study Bible*, (Nashville, TN: Holman Bible Publishers), 1968.

14 *HCSB Study Bible*, (Nashville, TN: Holman Bible Publishers), 1976.

15 *HCSB Study Bible*, (Nashville, TN: Holman Bible Publishers), 1978, 2018

16 *HCSB Study Bible*, (Nashville, TN: Holman Bible Publishers), 1644.

LAW-KEEPING
DUTY
OBLIGATION
PERFORMANCE
WORKS
RELIGION
ATTENDANCE
RULES

There's so much more to Jesus than this. Perfect attendance, perfect performance—none of it works. Dead, dry rule keeping keeps us from embracing this simple promise: We are fully known and deeply loved. Join Bethke for a 6-week study as he unpacks the differences between teeth gritting and grace, law and love, performance and peace, despair and hope.

lifeway.com/jesusisgreater
800.458.2772 | LifeWay Christian Stores

JESUS > RELIGION
THE BIBLE STUDY
JEFFERSON BETHKE

ALSO FOR ADULTS!

LifeWay | Adu